HERE'S PERMISSION
Volume 1

Poetry from 2004 - 2014

Zellia E. Fossett

Copyright © 2014 Zellia E. Fossett

All rights reserved. No part of this book may be reproduced in any form or by any means, electronic or mechanical, including photo-copying, recording, or by any information storage and retrieval system, without written permission from the author. This excludes a reviewer who may quote brief passages in a review.

Edited by: Pamela Davis

Cover Design: Kimberly Gaston

Published by G Publishing, LLC

Library of Congress Control Number: 2014920199

ISBN: 978-0-9862379-0-4

Printed in the United States of America

For anyone who has ever added to… or taken away from my definition of love. Thank you.

Contents

Temporal Formication	6
High school	7
o AA	9
Vitamin D	11
dear Santita	12
That's what your love is (Mom)…	14
Detroit	15
For MLK	16
Brown Sugar	19
If racism…	22
The levees	25
What you think you know	29
Undo	30
In Store	31
Gettin' me together	32
A Waste…	33
A permanent salutation	37
Recluse intervals of life	38
Mid-August	39
BFF Allegiance	41
Life	42
forgiveness	44
The One	48
Give her paper	50
Fatigue	51
Enchantment	52
I love you like…	53
Love's Logic	55
Lillianthevalley	56
What happens when Cupid lies…	58
In and on my mind	59
I'm no poet	61
So lovely	62
Lessons Learned	64
Adulthood	66
Worth studying	67
We Rest Easy	68

"4:37 a.m." 69
Danseur Silhouette.. 70
Doppelganger 71
Her white heat 72
Hot and bothered (both good things)........................ 73
The people mover... 74
If I can't have you…... 75
Last night... 77
Epilogue... 78

Temporal Formication

The world's on pins and needles now,
That's always how it seems.
Many more needles than pins somehow.
Lilies close and actors bow.
We mustn't say what we mean.
The world's on pins and needles now,
Poverty stronger than law should allow.
Bums hope for new dreams.
Loving more needles than pins somehow.
The snow is much too heavy for the plow.
To fight the flood, form a team.
The world's on pins and needles now,
Empty the safe, rape the cow.
Cheese, buttermilk and cream.
Many more needles than pins somehow.
For your mood swings, a voodoo doll,
There is no skin left to clean.
The world's on pins and needles now,
Many more needles than pins somehow.

High school

What a skyscraper of memories.
My brain was growing
in the middle of downtown
and I fell in love
with books and
women.
And I felt ashamed of both loves.
Making the honor roll
was the thing to do
in my crew
and skipping class
always felt better
in retrospect
than it ever did
in real life.
What a position to be in…
young and full of
energy that was years old.
When they started
tearing bricks down,
they made memories
invisible and the
outline of the architecture
stood still in my mind.
What we take away
from our free education
we continuously unveil
with age, in the most
unpredictable slices in time.
Then
my obstacle was high school
and I never really met a challenge.
I never learned much
I did not already know.

Except for advanced placement calculus.
I did learn how to learn though.
And so, exceptionally well…

o   AA

As a minority group
African Americans
May often feel that
The very essence
Of every detail of their lives
Is *minor*
In the eyes of others.
In the bigger picture of
Life and hope and happiness
And the future.
In the system
Built of systems
That is America
Itself.
They have delegated
That one month's time
Is enough to
Learn our history,
Heritage…
Our legacy.
But how can thousands
Of years
Of ruling natural land,
Creating and molding humanity
Be thoroughly stuffed into
A
30 day repeat
Of only inventions
And world records?
What makes us
A strong and unique people
Is our dynamism.
Our passion and deep sense of
Ingenuity.

Our ability to render
All things
From life.
From earth.
Out of unimaginable circumstances
Even with no
Tomorrows
Promised.

Vitamin D

I've always
been fascinated
by sunlight.
It controls
our first move
every day.
It controls
the flow of traffic
in the city
and the number of bodies
at the beach.
There is power
in sunlight.
Enough to sustain
crop and population alike.
Enough to hold
Planet Earth upright
on its axis—decaying Ozone and all.
It shines energy
while shining warmth on us.

dear Santita

The true beauty of a woman is in her selflessness.
And in the sacrifices she folds over and keeps hidden in a box adjacent her king sized bed.
She finds brilliant joy when in company and great sorrow only when overcome by unwanted loneliness.
Her love works hard, unorthodox hours of overtime, through heat and winter weather.
She bears no concern for loves lost or those forced away by circumstance, only hopes that the *her* she has left is in well enough condition for the one who deserves all of her.
And her brain is immaculate, her complete soul similarly so.
She imagines daily a world without worry and stress and offers her back as stable support to the broken and those who have given up.
She cradles with gentle care and patience as plentiful as the grains of sand on a beach.
Her mere presence illustrates her worth.
She evokes positive energy from humans, animals and nature alike; humble always.
She searches for renewed purpose and refurbished passion after a storm of near successes.
She wakes up when the sun does and examines her curves and brown skin in a full length mirror.
She meditates, staying grounded while planting seeds of peace and forgiveness.
She ages in the most important ways.
Secret keeper. Memory maker. Organized, righteous, focused and emotional.
She cries when she needs to and dislikes having to need to.
Her breathing is what I breathe for and…
For me, she has always been enough.
She is the ideal mold to craft creation after.

First born because any later there'd be nothing but smoke and burning bridges.
Dear Santita, you are so soundly beautiful, my love.

That's what your love is (Mom)…

Vital, breath-giving, emotion-stirring, act-right-prompting.
Eyes on the back of your head.
A tasteful account of "been-there-done-that".
Relentless humor and blunt honesty.
Knowing the truth, even when I try my best to hide it.
A higher power moving through you as you forgive and reshape.
Spending time doing exactly what you want to be doing.
Obsessed with details and accessories and all the ways to bring beauty closer to the reality of things.
A memory bank made of cast iron, with some rust the color of copper, here and there… and yet the most important events preserved and readily accessible.
Like every day is for celebrating, with great music and delicious food.
Like my favorite soup on a day when there's a negative temperature outside.
Like a tree with branches bearing fruit with me in mind.
Molding, protecting, consoling, reassuring.
Built for the fall and prepared to get right back up.
Indefatigable…
That's what your love is…

Detroit

A jagged rock cut from the American boulder.
Stretched out like water does across the river view.
Mixed and matched and chopped up, trying to get screwed
back together…
By carpenters with no depth of perception and
Voters who are illiterate and heartless and hungry for the
money it does not have.
Hot in July
and cold in January
and lukewarm
all the months
in between.
Undefined zodiac
of space
on a globe
that merely list it
in top ten rosters
for violence
and where not
to raise a family.
Supported by
faithful news reporters;
betrayed by its
political leaders.
Loved and
Dazzling…
Overcast and
Doleful…
Deserted when it wants to be.
A portrait hanging crooked on a never-ending wall
That outlines a motorized mitten of madness.
…Bedlam colored by construction…

For MLK

Even little kids were saying,
"I'll follow him."
Purposed and fearless,
He marched through streets
And across bridges
And up and down the aisles of churches.
A fighter,
Without fists.
Father; his forte.
I speak of
A man whose rhetoric
Stood like mountains high,
For a chosen people
To climb to their peaks…
Seeking safety, love and peace.
…
A man whose courage
Enabled him to
Become a giant amongst dwarves.
Like Goliath,
He had shoulders
Holding the weight
Of many, many men.
All saying,
"Let's follow him."
Him.
The man
In the suit and tie.
The man
With courageous Coretta by his side.
The man who
Fought for freedom
And equality.
The man to whom I am

Indebted for
This liberal education
And all my
rides on public transit.
I'll follow him.
Back through the roads
Of Atlanta, Georgia.
Back to the yards where
Sanitation workers
Yelled and screamed and hoped
For liberty.
Back to the towns
On front lawns,
Where crosses burned
And much faith was lost.
They followed him.
He shed blood; gave his life
For a cause
He believed was
Greater than he alone.
He faced death
Yet still lives
In a legacy
Forever engraved in the
Souls of
Many, many men
Who followed him.
Orator, author,
Gifted writer of sacred scripture;
He survived the
Plague of
Political patriarchy
With style.
In '57 he gave us
The ballot.
And now we can vote

For whoever, whenever.
And in '63
We learned of
His dream.
One that is still unfolding
Before us.
In 1968
"I've been to the mountaintop"
Became the tangible manifestation
Of the essence
Of what will always be
a great man.
Reverend, activist, pioneer and hero.
A righteous leader, vessel of comfort
And a gifted revolutionary.
Laying prostrate before
A power
Mightier than all beings,
In prayer for a change
We know is soon to come.
Our president
Is his dream.
Our president
Is following him.

"Art must discover and reveal the beauty which prejudice and caricature have overlaid" – Alain Locke in his essay "The New Negro"

Brown Sugar

This bourgeoisie playpen has been glorified by zoot suits and women with gorgeous faces.

"Cotton-colored" girls, Owen Madden called the ones whose shadows left light-skinned traces.

We left the south for Chicago, Washington and this little place down in NYC.

Where our talents were embraced and our sense of doubt erased, but both to inadequate degrees.

Although black performers flourished, drenched in the spotlight provided by the Cotton Club,

They sacrificed an enormous amount of dignity for each check stub.

The luxury of the club's inside walls few Harlemites could ever afford.

So there was a white only audience with yes, you guessed it— all negroes on one accord.

Duke, it wasn't the melody and Ella, it wasn't the music that made those tunes complete.

But rather the swing and the jump of the jazz that lends harmony incapable of defeat.

A separate reality speaks to the renaissance born in our bellies and raised in our hearts.

The kind heavily documented in history books and not on billboard charts.

Brown Sugar, sweet but unrefined, was the quality of the art that the Cotton Club combined.

This exclusive paradise is depicted by images of blacks; well-dressed and studio posing.

Cotton on the fact that this club owned our backs; a color line and Harlem, Madden was juxtaposing.

Whites ran the club—produced, wrote and choreographed every single one of its shows.

While we entertained, cooked, waited, bussed tables and cleaned whatever we were told.

Our talent is worth more than every penny that was spent in that club and other uptown spaces.

Bars, food and "tall, tan, terrific" women could be found anywhere, they came there to see our faces.

For without our expertise the word on the streets would not have been all about the cotton.

The 100% realness of those events and the thickness of the thread we haven't forgotten.

Ethel Waters stitched "Stormy Weather" into a lyrical quilt, blanketed over by Garland, Armstrong, Sinatra and Holiday.

75 other artists followed in her groove, singing a song written first for Cab Calloway.

Malvin Gray Johnson, William H. Johnson, Aaron Douglas, Zora and Langston Hughes.

John Coltrane, Ma Rainey, Bessie Smith, Minnie Riperton and Charlie Patton too.

Brown Sugar, sweet and unrefined. Like syrup… robust like fermented wine was the quality of the art that the Cotton Club combined.

This noble neck tied nightspot had a maximum capacity of 700 heads.

Through lips, hips and even fingertips music, film, dance, poetry, painting and photography were bred.

Let the positive elements of that history repeat themselves, just like we learned to let freedom ring.

Let the fact that money was made as our talents were displayed be the token of every linguistic string.

Categorized under a tab where prestige cannot be confined.

Even if they were blind and we were Braille they couldn't find…

a sensation comparable to what the Cotton Club combined.

If racism...

If racism was a natural disaster, it'd tear our limbs from our bodies, in a whirlwind of fluid hate, broken hope and would create horrific memories.

And if it were man-made its design would grow out of control, possessing generations, one after the next, of inherently evil souls unable to reason.

If racism were a season it'd be the coldest yet. Strong enough to burst pipes, alienate races of creatures, freeze bodies still... glorify cold terrain.

And if it were a disease it'd move gracefully up the spines of millions of backs, like tiny bugs permeating the brain within a matter of seconds; causing sores, leaving scars, killing.

If racism were a sin it'd be the greatest on the list of seven, promoting hierarchy and individual superiority, the best friend of pride.

A criminal. Notorious. Causing newspaper stands to flood. Unstoppable, like the banking beauties Bonnie and Clyde. Mastermind, like Iago, turning them against us and us against ourselves.

A fire. Like the great one in Chicago in 1871. Relentless, self-sufficient, destroying whole towns, families, hearts and history books.

If racism were an addict it'd find relief in vulgar obscenities and irrational behavior. It'd meet us on the edge where our anger makes everything blurry and hard to understand.

And if it were footwear, it'd be born of antiquity. Stitched with persecution, nailed together to support a corroded nation, painted over with a stroke of every color known.

If racism were a magazine, the percentage of subscribers would be as fat as…

A hippo's ass
An aggravated pimple
A sumo wrestler's shadow
The Clumps on Sunday…

As fat as…
Big Boy on steroids or
The sound of Biggie Smalls inhaling…

The percentage would be as fat as the bead of sweat that rolled from Bush's forehead when Obama won. Faithful and fruitful subscribers we'd all be, praising its pages in song and deed.

And if racism were a marathon it'd be awarded a seven page layout in the Guinness Book of World Records, longest period of bullshit acceptance in the U. S. of A.

If it were an art form it'd be practiced by 150 creative chapters and 8,000 maniac members, most of whom live in Genesee County, ready to suit up in their pointy white hoods and ride on horses.

Death. It'd be slow and undeserving. It'd be buried in a casket covered in karma, a word with many relative definitions.

If racism were alive and well we'd see it everywhere we turn. In our homes, at school and at work and even in church.

We'd all find ourselves in necessary forums for very necessary discourse in efforts to bring forth necessary change.

We must congregate and organize or we will…

Be swallowed by the tsunami it becomes
And damaged by its miracle potion gone bad.
We'll be trapped under the icebergs of its arctic effects
While watching it dress itself in patriotic plaid.

Racism cultivates fear and like religion, it convicts souls. It will leave us all politically imprisoned for life.
We'll fiend for injustice and shoot ignorance into our veins, find shoes that don't fit and take inequality as our lawfully wedded wife.

We find ourselves in necessary forums… for very necessary discourse… in efforts to bring forth necessary change.

The levees

When the levees in
Our souls break,
Love will cover the lands
As far as our eyes
Will let us see.
Erupting waters of emotions
Will pour out of our
Hands and mouths
Damn near effortlessly.
Cover us from head to toe,
East, west,
Over here and most definitely
Over there.
Where people are steady dying,
And kids too,
Fuck crying –
Cause that's not getting us anywhere.
People are wishing
They were at least American.
And for what,
To sit at the bottom of this bucket
They keep calling
A pot?
Yea, because sadly enough
This busted bucket is more
Than they've currently got.
Their governments have failed them,
Mixed them all up,
Misspelled their names
And abandoned them in fields
That are ditch, dark black.
We though, full of meat and potatoes,
Good sense and plump tomatoes,
Will stuff our "sorry" in a sack

And help them find their way back—
Home, where real live
Love plants are grown.
And no one's good at keeping track
Of all the
Bad seeds you've sewn.
Where nothing is ever blown
Out of proportion.
Women so malnourished
They pass children
Like they do urine;
While American girls
Run off to get abortions.
I don't quite
Remember exactly,
When I became a journalist
That hates the news.
I imagine though,
That it was around the same time
Everyone began singing the
"why are we at war?" blues.
Every day I watch more
Sad shit than I do good,
Saying if only we could…
Not realizing that indeed we can.
When I see anchors smiling,
Like they're in a commercial for coke,
Like all isms are jokes,
I know the concept of news
They don't fully understand.
They just report it and
We sit back and snort it
Until off of grief we get
Really, really high.
Put their brains inside of birds
And I bet backwards

Is the direction those little
Birdies would fly.
"Save developing nations"
Reigns at the top of
My list of things to do.
And when December comes
Almighty plump ole Santa
Better name it top priority too.
And if he doesn't
We can act like he wasn't
Serious
Or that it slipped his mind.
Or we can wrap our revelry
In a bow
Or in the sticks you break then watch glow,
And give it away
In short amounts of time.
The cost of our dollar menu items
Equal the same amount
As the wages they get paid in a day.
They wake up to
Cold sunrise,
Go to sleep without good music, television
Or even a bed on which to lie.
These people
Are our people,
For we are all one race.
The words of Bob Marley
We must not forget.
Don't worry about a thing,
Stomp hard to this beat of hope
Like you have the feet of a disciplined cadet.
It is this evidence
Of our passion for peace
That needs to be covered in the news.
Who the fuck do I need to train?

To grab a mic and admit that
They're fighting for, fully becoming
And expecting that change.
When the levees in
Our souls break,
Love will cover the lands
As far as our eyes
Will let us see.
Let the levees of your soul break
And watch love pour out
Damn near incessantly.

What you think you know

All you know…
about a person…
is what they allow you
to know.
Somehow we can control a milli-fraction of perception.

Undo

If only things
could be undone
just as easily
as they are done.
And if there were
a button to push
or strict pathways to take,
would we ever learn
from our missteps
and fast hands?

In Store

Nothing can be a secret… ever… totally.
I shake my head
and add us to the list
of things I once wanted.
With your promises that make me feel
as empty as your excuses do.
With your cigarettes
and your fifth of filth.
You remind me
the days of writing love letters
are far gone.
The way you look at me
like we never met before
makes me happy I never gave you
what you thought was in store.

Gettin' me together

I'm tipping the ashtray
every time I think of you.
Smoking away
until I can't
control the direction of my thoughts.
I puff, wait and drag
and watch the air around me
twist into white swirls.
Dimensional clouds begging me
to tell the truth.
Flowing through my hair,
tugging at my locs,
trying to read me.
Hell, I don't know
if I've ever let anyone
as close as this smoke
I let in…
And on…
And through me…
This, that I do as daily as I wish
I were doing you
is all I know.
This reflection.
This culmination of days passed
and journals filled.
This ode is composed
of the only notes
I know to sing.
I want to be
in the right key…
While I'm getting' myself together.

A Waste...

One day at work
a guy
called me
beautiful…
then
a stud…
and then
a waste
of a woman.
I wonder
what part
of me
I am "wasting"
by deciding
not to
have a
man's child
or be a
man's partner.
It certainly
cannot be
my heart.
I know
for sure
that it
is not
my brain
that's "wasting" away.
I do not
feel some
unforeseen void
in my womb.
I am
not craving

the scent
of cologne
or a voice
deep in tone.
I do not
feel drawn
to the ease
of letting
patriarchy
pave my way
to retirement.
I wear
my pants baggy
because I like
the way
it feels.
I enjoy
the space
between
the material
and my skin…
the space
between
the illusion
of my
physical make up
and the reality
of how slim
I actually
am.
Just because
I wear
baggy clothes
does not
mean that
I am

not sexy
or that
I do not
see myself
as such.
Just because
my body
is not
on display
under
fitted clothes
of your forte
does not
mean that
I do not
know the worth
underneath
my baggy
ones.
I briefly
fought with
why he'd
dare say
such a thing
to me.
Then I
stopped…
because
only a fool
would call
a woman
a waste.
It has
been said
that …
"a man is only as strong as the woman who holds him".

So
how strong
might I be,
a woman
holding onto
another woman?
How
healing
and soothing
is the touch
of my caress
then?
How is it
that my voice
in darkness
feels
just as soft
and secure
as it does
in light?
How is it
that when men
look
at women
they begin again?
… The only thing
that's been
wasted here…
is his breath.

A permanent salutation

This...
on my skin...
is detached from a human figure.
It is its own existence.
It draws significance and definition
from a specific moment in time
in my life
when I was loved on hundreds of pages
and in every other way
I needed to be.
I was too young (and didn't know even then)
to know that was how I'd want to be
loved for the rest of my life.
This...
on my skin...
is the mark of true love.
Unconditional, and just barely educated
about the troubles of this world.

Recluse intervals of life

Sometimes you have to find your way back to yourself.
And sometimes that's hard when you don't know when or where exactly you became a different you.
You can…
Find yourself
in negative strips of flashbacks
and broken English.
In stacks of newspapers.
In solitude.
In confession.
In the lead of number two pencils with worn out erasers.
In aromas of
yesterdays gone.
Experience yourself in midnight songs,
With tear stained pillows counting sheep for you.
You can…
Find yourself
in the most vulnerable
seconds and scenes.
At the bullshit in between.
Where you trust yourself to be.
Where you trust yourself to be.
Where you trust yourself to be…
Is where you can always find yourself.
Or a good segment of who you have become.

Mid-August

Fall means dressing in layers
Or in clothes from
Different seasons.
The sky changes color,
Flowing with the mood
Of the trees
And the leaves tell the clouds
How low to settle.
The smell outside
Makes
Childhood feel only
A thought or two away.
That first day…
red backpack…
recess…
hot lunches and cold bag lunches…
innocent crushes on smart people…
field trips
and half days.
Fall means finding peace
In quiet corners
With warm drinks.
It is the only season
That I find myself
Remembering love lost.
It is the only season
I use to put my life in perspective
And accept
How old I am in real life.
Fall means fresh donuts
And apple cider
And saying hello
to strangers in the park.
Sometimes we end up

Uncovering all the emotions
We stashed away in winter
And said were too heavy
To unpack during summer.
Fall is usually when everything
Feels just fine.
My mistakes seem more
Forgivable.
My next move seems
More pivotal.
It means we can catch our breath
With the window open and
Feel a breeze that has muscles.

BFF Allegiance

The sooner we understand
that loyalty is a choice,
the better off
our hearts will be.
And the sooner
we understand how our hearts
are more likely inclined
to operate,
the more responsibility
we can take
for our own feelings.
I have found myself
over extended
in some matters of the heart,
only to realize
that I am
my own savior.
We have to
always love ourselves
the most
and know when
to make moves
that prove
we know this to be true.
Friendship is like
tying shoe strings.
Sometimes
they
come
loose.

Life

Mistakes
and decisions…
People say
every move
you make
is your call
and whatever
you want
to happen
with your life
can definitely
happen…
just…
work steady…
and focus your energy
in the right
directions.
Hear me out, Life.
Since when
do populations
live on Earth
and spend
so much of their
lifetimes
thinking, worrying
or playing around
with money?...
While you
just pass us by…
Life...
Allow us
free time
and space
to just be.

Make
capitalism
and consumerism
choices…
instead of
disguising them
as a lifestyle.
Go easy on us
sometimes…
since you know
there's no
pause button
on your console…
and there's never
been a manual…
maybe there are
a few
cheat codes.
Growth and change
are vined around
tomorrow's forecast.
Step when I step, Life.
Start to see me
as more than
the list of numbers
the government tracks.
Respect me.

forgiveness

only lovers go there.
they clear space
to make room
for memorabilia
and they stack
what used to be
in boxes,
to the ceiling. They
organize residual
emotions
in the attics
of their hearts
and in the empty seconds
between thoughts
and thickening silence.
for years
the storage
settles into itself—
a vessel of
failing fortitude
standing tall.
they crack windows
and
lightly dust
the ill mansion
of a residence,
searching the
halls for what
their pride
has hidden.
only lovers
visit and revisit
the boxes
and pretend to

review the contents.
when all around them
is darkness,
the sun interrupts
the night
in a rush
to give them a
new day
to clear
their
attics.
Lonely sends them up
into themselves
and they
search their hearts
and there in
the light
is all they
hid away in
shaded, shadowed
hallways of
their love.
to reflect.
to grow.
to change.
to forgive.
We ask ourselves if
love
needs
space.

I don't know if I've been writing about love for so long because I needed it, wanted it or if it was because learning the meaning of love is a lifetime lesson. I've defined and redefined, created and edited, speculated and erased—just trying to figure it out. I have succeeded and failed in relationships, all the while believing in the power of love itself. The power it has to heal and to forgive. The power it has that makes us want to change ourselves and actually begin the changes. Love, in all the different ways I experience it, has taught me so much about who I am and about my capabilities and capacities.

When someone you love starts loving someone else it sometimes feels like they never loved you at all. Your deepest emotions become questionable and the thought of intimacy between the two of you is painful… when not that long ago it made you smile wide. It's amazing really—the power of human emotion. It moves us to the most beautiful fulfillment of dreams and too, the cruelest acts of rage.

The love that we give to our family members and friends is different from the love we may have for a significant other, but only because the customs, boundaries and expectations change. The word itself having so many meanings… "love" is misused and abused and misinterpreted. People don't know what love is… they have defined it along the lines of great sex or good compatibility… they look for it on sale and in the monogram prints of name brands. They feel like they order it custom made with their new cars and mansions built up from the ground.

Love encompasses every part of speech. Love always rests in the details.

Love is…you. What we mean to say is that "love is you". It is what you do and don't do that define the word 'love' when you say "I love you" to someone. In a simply complicated way, we give of our literal selves when we give love. What happens when two individuals feel they are compatible is that their definitions of love are exercised and expressed in the same ways and so they believe one another—for years upon years the union strengthens with conviction. Love is discernment in the way that it empowers you to make *soul decisions* that are the best for your *heart*, all while you bear magnificent sacrifices.

Finding a mate shouldn't be a life goal and failed relationships don't translate into personal failure. So love is to be had and not to be found and your life is about **you and your happiness** and not about other people who come in and out of it. I have found happiness in self improvement, in intimacy and in the destitute nights I've spent documenting theories, descriptions, snapshots, remnants and definitions of love.

I always fall for women who like their eggs over easy…

The One

Most people sing in the shower
or wash their hair.
I stand there washing and
imagine what you might
look like…
Where you're going to
just up and appear from.
Imagine you
touching my neck
just the way
I like my neck
to be touched.
Imagine you
knowing me
like I know adlibs.
Singing me under your breath.
The lather coats me
and the steam rises
with my desire
to know you.
To be where you are.
Where ever it is
that you are.
Sometimes I sing
but only
when it feels right.
I search my heart beat,
stepping into the
fountain above my head.
I wash away
the agony of
not yet having
met you.
I rinse off the exhaust

of wondering
if you even know I live.
I step out into today
and try to clear my head of you…
and how amazing you are.
Where ever it is
that you are.

Give her paper

Won't you
write this woman a love letter?
She really
needs to read one.
She looks at me
as though she's never seen
love let loose on leafed paper,
made for the pen's blood.
She acts as though
she's never
read love aloud.
So… open…
she must always be alone
to feel safe enough to breathe deeply.
Impress her
with your penmanship.
Persuade her with romantic prose
and gravid poetry.
With your words
let her know
that there is more to be had.

Fatigue

I'm sweating
on the inside.
Nervous for your touch.
I have weakened fantasies
of you and me
doing innocent things.
Slowly and free
of second guesses
and regrets…
We will wrap ourselves
in the skin of our yesterdays
and cuddle
and share heat.
Surely…
just as sure as Jah blesses,
we will sink into the slumber
of our dreams and
make love a new shape.

Enchantment

Attraction
has a feel to it.
It's sort of like a
summer breeze
that interrupts—
timely and
at the right angle,
for the right amount of time.
It grabs your attention.
It brings immediate relief.
If only nonverbal
could become
spoken language...

I love you like...

I love you more than NBA players love cheating on their wives
More than honey bees love the queen in the center of the hive
And I'm alive and breathing and at your feet the second you call
Some say love's a losing game and for you I'd risk it all
I love you like addicts love dreaming of being sober
More than Jonah loved his maker after it was all over
And you barely even notice when you make me lose my breath or next thought
Knowing good and well it's more than my attention you've caught
I love you more than pimps love to count dollars
More than the probability that a high school valedictorian will become a collegiate scholar
And there are no chains to break free from for I am not bound
Just mesmerized and struck frozen every time you come around
I love you deep like the anger you feel sitting in traffic on I-94
Deep like the itch of a healing sore or the gaze of a man's stare at the football score
No more can I contain and manage pretending that I'm okay
When I'm dangling off of the tip of your tongue with every word you say
I love you more than the world loves Michael Jackson's music and dance moves
More than Jill Scott loves to serve a lover who puts it down the best breakfast foods
And your groove is strong enough to undo my zipper, always draws attention to us in the club

I'd give a whole week's worth of time for just one second
of your love
I love you like full time cashiers love exact change
And don't think that these feelings will stay the same
I promise, I love you more each day
A love fancier than fairy tales and real in every way

Love's Logic

May I touch you,
while I synthesize
the surprise you are?
Disentangle the woo
you do.
My fingertips
memorizing your slim.
May I caress you
to rub away
your past?
Massage you
high into the sky
of today?
Touch you like
it's the first time,
every time.
No,
like it's
the only time.
Such regalia,
your body on mine.
Did I
feel you quiver?
Feel the goose bumps
race like zippers
up your spine?
May I make sense
of what
you do to me?

Lillianthevalley

Your devotion
is welcome.
Its sweet smell
and its roots
spreading wide
across the land.
A soul of wonder
and blighted freedom.
On the sideline
of love
and in defense
of it all.
Mourning dew
from yesterday's hours
just before sunrise.
Blooming…
only to droop
and let all the
anguish drip.
Your devotion
is welcome.
Its color washed pale
and its weight
seemingly light.
Eyes that have
watched snow melt away
and constellations
shift time in space.
Mornings
of
Sundays
reconciled.
Touching…
only for a little while.

Lillianthevalley…
Those stems are pathways to mounded secrets.
Those leaves are proof of the pain.
The flowers keep the good and bad even.
You are someone's bright, morning star. *
Believe me…
Your devotion
is welcome.

*William Charles Fry. *The Lily of the Valley*. 1881.

What happens when Cupid lies...

I'm
all filled up.
All worn out
over you.
Up to my limit
with impassioned fury.
Pacing the floors
of my heart
for every base board
you've knocked loose.

In and on my mind

I have this
soft spot
for you…
in my mind.
I want to
lay you down
in it and…
make love
to you.
Love
like you've never
felt before.
I want you
to be
disoriented…
in the down comforters
and Egyptian cotton
of my imagination.
I want you to be
torn…
between deciding
whether to never leave
or always stay…
here with me.
I want you
overcome by
the thought of me.
Pupils glazed over
by the fervor
of our dreamland.
Psyche exhausted
by the
potentiality too.
And as soon as you

obtain entry
at the door
of my heart,
I will gladly
lead you to
that soft spot
I have for you…
in my mind.

I'm no poet

It was the eggs over easy, the way your brain embellished life, the peace signs, red lights and long roads, the pillows soaked upon your departure, the solace that attached itself to your smile, the underwear with the monkeys on them, the internal bleeding and hemorrhaging of the hood you both know, the family, the feminists, the activists, dreams of New York, the paint and the fresh fruit, the kaleidoscope cut-out that you were, the creativity you moved and shook, the perpetuation of what used to be, the depression consumed by the warm months of summer, illegality of it all, illegitimacy of that union, the jokes you two owned, the fabrics patented, loneliness, passion, wishes for better feelings, glue, crayons, ink and how you made it all come together—stamping her identity with nostalgia and just like war photographs, making the pain help her recall all the right words to explain the nonsense.

So lovely

What's
safe to say
now?...
That I still
miss you
after all these years?
Is it
safe to say
that I'm sorry
lying seemed
better than leaving
at the time?...
I remember you
freestyling in the car
when we were
on our way
to Meijer.
I remember
being so happy
and that happiness
containerizing
all ill feelings…
I remember
some of the best art
coming out of me
when we loved.
Is it okay
that I miss
the muse in you?...
Is it
safe to say
that I still think
of you and us
sometimes?...

The same pain
I caused you
rested in my spirit
after all was
said and done…
The same pain
you tried to bury
in tunes about
Holly Grove in New Orleans.
My love is
different
now
and
"I'm all healed up".
And you…
I bet you are
still
so
lovely.
It feels like
nothing
is safe
to say.
Then again,
the words
would only
drift in the space
that separates us still
and I'd sit here…
with bad memories
of a lovely woman.

Lessons Learned

When I wanted
you to feel jealous
because I thought
it would increase
the feeling of me
being loved.
I always thought
I was so jealous
of your ex-lovers-turned-friends
because I loved you
so much.
When you left
Donny Hathaway's music
pushed me to the edge
of heartache.
When you came back
it was just
too late
because I was already
in pieces…
too many pieces.
I'm rubbing oil
over old scars
that have
raised my skin
when I write
about you.
You taught me
that to love
is not to own,
for we give our heart
to those we want
to have it—freely.
You taught me

the significance
of choice
and how to
find the power
that's within the reality
of having
been chosen.
You taught me
that committing to someone
should never equate
to a loss of privacy.
You taught me
that my lies
were only salt.
You taught me
how to mold and hem
my androgyny
and to embrace
all that is feminine
about my nature.
You taught me
the importance
of vulnerability
and saying exactly
what I want to say.
You taught me
the malleability
and breathlessness
that love can have
when you let it.
And all of those
were hard lessons
for me
to learn then.

Adulthood

She's grown.
Into the heels she dreamed of fitting.
Into the roles she kept forgetting she was made for
and in timing perfect enough to bypass her complaints.
She's grown.
Out of low self perspectives.
Out of needing help from the collective
and dishes out depth and definition for her claims.
She's grown.
Up and through clouds.
Like a bean stalk or a mile long trail
through a tale of the sky.
New job and new car
on the same distant roads
of Illinois.
Like she controls the train's arrival.
Can't tell her nothin'.
Controls the departure too.
Man, has she grown.

Worth studying

She tells me…
I'm worth
creeping for.
She tells me…
I'm the answer
worth cheating for.
I say to her…
that I am worth
being the
single subject.
I say to her…
I am
worth studying.

We Rest Easy

It starts to rain
and she hops up
to open
her bedroom window
and let the
sound in.
And let the
smell in.
She knows
I love rain.
She does too.
When she climbs
back in bed
our doubled silverware mold
holds more heat
than it did before.
The rain doesn't slow up
until I'm
fast asleep,
under the spell
of the dropping beads…
and under
the warmth
of her right thigh.
As it rains,
we rest easy…

"4:37 a.m."

This morning
I sifted through
the mental stash of memories
of you
leftover in me.
I wanted to feel
you on me,
watch your body respond to
my touch.
I wanted to feel how
I first felt
when I saw you;
So overwhelmed
that all I could do was stare.
And so damn curious
that my
every movement
was gentle
so as not to chase you away.

Danseur Silhouette

I miss the way
you'd kiss me
and how I could
hear how hard
you wanted me
in your breath
and feel how bad
you wanted me
in the pressure
of the push
of your lips.
Missing the way
your hands
held onto my neck,
both sides real soft.
You
moved me
and moved through me
like pulses of light
on the dance floor
of some techno joint.
You still do…
sometimes…
when I let myself
let you.

Doppelganger

I know you're
out there…
busy…
searching for another me.
And you know
there's only one
so I'm not sure
why you bother.
Maybe you've got hope
that you can
transform
that little someone
on your arm
into someone that
resembles me.
Or maybe you've got
Magic...
But you
can't replicate a soul…

Her white heat

Her shirt is yellow
like this sheet of paper.
Her heart loves
real hard
like mine.
No other colors
on her,
I remember…
And I recognize
the hue has changed
in my world.
Need not be heard…
see those footsteps
and you want to
look back…
and harder.
I maneuver closer to her…
With my fingertips
in the day time
And my
whole hands
at night.
I stand affected…
even by her shadow…
And by the white heat
she leaves a trail of…

Hot and bothered (both good things)

I'd never
heard my name
sound so sweet
until it came
from within her
and out of
her mouth.
Suspended
in coils of sound,
I'd never
heard my name
said with
so much meaning.
When she colored
around the lines
of the letters,
I felt chosen…
like the single utensil
out of a box
of thousands.
Her skin became
a bright, blushing red.
She moaned…
without regard
for surroundings
and held tight
without the same.
I was both
hot and bothered…
which are both
good things.

The people mover

Her love
is a locomotive.
I wonder
if she's
ever been
to anyone else
all of what
she is to me.
When other people
look at her,
do they see
all that I see?
She
dimensionalizes beauty
right before my eyes…
She
transports positivity
through the city.
Her love is
a healing railway…
inspiring graffiti hands
and using
fragments of faith
and shards of ambition
to decorate
the future.

If I can't have you…

I find myself
engrossed
in daydreams
of the way
it felt to
kiss you.
The things
you'd do
with your
tongue.
The way
you'd tease
my lips
with yours.
That sound
you'd make
when it
got good
to you…
unbearably
good to you.
I miss you
for private reasons
and for some
that I
cannot explain.
I caught myself
biting the knuckle
of my pointer finger
on my left hand…
thinking about
the last time
I saw you…
and the time

before that too.
I wonder
if you used to
thirst for me
the way
I did for you.
If I can't
have you...
I will settle
for these
reminiscent daydreams
because...
they almost
feel just as
glorious.

Last night

…I had
a dream
about you.
You were
dishing out
compliments
one after
the other.
I was blushing
on and off.
You said that…
it felt good…
and that…
it smelled
good like
you'd imagined.
You said that…
it made you
want more,
pointing to the
space between
my thighs.
Last night
I had a
dream
about you.
When I looked
between
my thighs
to see your
new found love…
there was
my first novel…
New, golden and glowing…

Epilogue

Something this natural must be right. Looking back, I've always been this way. I was a quiet, private… somewhat secretive child. Always watching, listening, absorbing, writing. I filled pages with pictures, rumors, truths, wishes, stories or my weekend plans. I questioned things in my journals and with my imagination in turbo mode, I sketched inventions too. I recorded phrases from my mother's phone conversations or parental pillow talk through the vents. I took notes in church and doodled during car rides. I remember drawing people's belongings that stood out to me – a leopard print backpack or a tie with a cool design on it. I've always given my undivided self to specifics. On holidays and for birthdays I was always gifted notebooks and diaries…that still happens today… and writing is all I know.

One of the most amazing facts about writing is that "it comes and goes and always stays". Rather than call the period of time when I am not writing a drought, a cave-sized absence or writer's block, I've come to understand it as the nature of the beast. Finalizing the decision to compile a book has been a journey itself because writing is so personal. I've accessed areas of my memory bank I never knew existed! At times, inspiration is an integral factor of my happiness as a writer and other times it's simply a matter of me saying what I feel in my heart to say and it miraculously coming out beautiful somehow. Writing has increased my brain's capacity for memory. It has helped me reason, interpret socialization and fight isolation. I owe it my sanity.

Like most people, the best of me comes out as I survive extreme emotions. Some five years ago, my significant other perused my journal and left a note (original, handwritten note printed on the cover of this book) that read "[Curiosity] got the best of me." It was left in place to mark an entry I'd written about them, of course. I felt betrayed, yes, but above all I felt... desirable. I felt like what I had to say must have been too good to turn away from. After all, it had been sought out and consumed all in one sitting! In collecting the first volume, I thought to pay tribute to that incident by allowing readers the *permission* to read my pages of poetry. Although not printed in chronological order, the poems were written between the ages of fourteen and twenty five. Furthermore, they are expressions and beliefs from various stages of my life.

If I had to name my top three favorite poems from this collection, I'd say "High School", "forgiveness" (purposefully printed in grayscale) and "Lessons Learned". On page 46, I ramble on about my thoughts on love and composing that was freeing. My friends always interrupt me in conversation or when I give advice and tell me that I need to "write that $#@* down!" So here I go! I'm writing things down! It is my hope that of all I have to say, everyone who turns the pages will close them and have taken away something or fully identified with an emotion I conveyed through words.

Through meditation and patience, ups and downs and missed turns... I have admitted... I have forgiven... I write.

I am a writer. And when people ask me why I am the way I am, all I can say is that I've always been this way. All I can say is that I'm me.

www.ingramcontent.com/pod-product-compliance
Lightning Source LLC
Chambersburg PA
CBHW031210090426
42736CB00009B/866